THE KINGDOM MANDATE HANDBOOK

Apostle Winston G. Baker

THE KINGDOM MANDATE HANDBOOK
Copyright ©2018 Winston G. Baker

ISBN 978-1506-912-02-8 PRINT
ISBN 978-1506-907-59-8 EBOOK

LCCN 2018966556

December 2018

Published and Distributed by
First Edition Design Publishing, Inc.
P.O. Box 20217, Sarasota, FL 34276-3217
www.firsteditiondesignpublishing.com

ALL RIGHTS RESERVED. No part of this book publication may be reproduced, stored in a retrieval system, or transmitted in any form or by any means — electronic, mechanical, photo-copy, recording, or any other — except brief quotation in reviews, without the prior permission of the author or publisher.

All scriptures quoted are from the King James Version of the Holy Bible.

*"The fruit of the righteous is a tree of life
and he that winneth souls is wise"*
Proverbs 11:30

Table of Contents

Introduction 7

Chapter 1 - WHY AM I HERE? The First Adam 9

Chapter 2 - WHY AM I HERE? The Last Adam 16

Chapter 3 - PURPOSE... 27

Chapter 4 - POWERFUL PRAYERS 39

Chapter 5 - ACTION TIME The Great Commission 42

Chapter 6 - READINESS TIPS.. 55

Chapter 7 - THE GOOD NEWS 62

Chapter8 - ALTAR WORKERS... 67

Chapter 9 - BYWAYS AND HEDGES 90

Chapter 10 - CONDUCT OF CHRIST'S AMBASSADORS... 99

Introduction

To God be the glory, great and mighty things He has done!

With a heartful of gratitude, I humbly present the 'Kingdom Mandate Handbook'. This third tool which God has directed me to prepare for all His kingdom citizens focuses on our mission as Christ's Ambassadors; and answers the question

'Why Am I Here'.

Every believer should know that they are called by Jesus Christ for a specific purpose, and as such, this tool, will guide them into confidently establishing their purpose in the kingdom of God and having it fulfilled. It is, therefore, my earnest expectation that believers once convicted of their purpose will confidently pursue it with passion.

It is inevitable! Once our purpose has been established and we begin to fulfil it, the kingdom of God will forcefully advance. Together we will pull men from the kingdom of darkness into the kingdom of God and colonize the earth; as we are representatives of our Lord and Saviour Jesus Christ.

Let's go Christ's Ambassadors!

Chapter 1

WHY AM I HERE?

The First Adam

This is without controversy, one of the most important questions an individual must answer in order to live a meaningful life. In answering this question, an individual establishes his or her purpose for being born. The answer to this question provides critical information for making some of life's major decisions.

What is my purpose?

What was I created for?

These questions are answered in the first chapter of the first book of the Bible, Genesis 1:26-28

> *And God said, Let Us make man in Our image, after Our likeness: and let them have dominion over the fish of the*

> *sea, and over the fowl of the air, and over the cattle, and over all the earth, and over every creeping thing that creepeth upon the earth.*
>
> *So, God created man in His own image, in the image of God created He him; male and female created He them.*
>
> *And God blessed them, and God said unto them, be fruitful, and multiply, and replenish the earth, and subdue it: and have dominion over the fish of the sea, and over the fowl of the air, and over every living thing that moveth upon the earth.*

Something moved in God's Spirit to make mankind and He –being a speaking Spirit- verbalized His thought to make man, in His image and after His likeness. So, man was created -as God said- in His image. This refers to the nature of God and includes: the ability to love, make decisions, judge and possess will power.

Man was also created after God's likeness and should, therefore, function in a similar manner as God. This is something we do by faith. The man made in God's nature, begins to operate as a speaking spirit too. God then decided to give this man dominion over fish, birds, animals and every creeping thing. That includes the earth and all its resources. Man is therefore ultimately in charge of everything that moves in the earth.

That was God's plan for mankind; for man to think and function like Him. Having dominion would establish him as a king or ruler over everything in the earth realm.

Eventually, the time came for God's purpose for mankind to be revealed. He made them in His image and likeness and set them as rulers. God's plan was not arbitrary. He had a reason for all He did, hence the reason He made man. We are not after-thoughts! We were placed on the earth for a specific reason.

This is our mandate! This is what man is expected to do.

What? Why? You ask eagerly. God reveals it in Genesis 1:28:

> *And God blessed them, and God said unto them, BE FRUITFUL, and MULTIPLY, and REPLENISH the earth.*

Man's first instruction and number one purpose therefore is to BE FRUITFUL. What exactly did God mean when He gave Adam the command to be fruitful? It is more than reproducing by giving birth to boy or girl babies. When God told Adam to be fruitful, He was a sinless being. He was in God's image and functioning like God. In fact, God was commanding Adam to produce other sinless beings.

God's message to Adam was that he should produce men like himself. Do you know why? The answer is quite simple, but the implementation is globally impacting! When Adam began to produce others like himself- without sin, powerful, full of the glory of God and the anointing- the kingdom of God that resided with Adam would ultimately fill the earth. The earth would eventually be filled or 'colonized' with sons of God, creating a reflection of heaven.

The term 'colonize' may be defined as:

The action or process of settling among and establishing control over indigenous people of an area; **or**
The action of appropriating a place or domain for one's own use.

A brief look at the history of the Caribbean region, reveals that prior to the arrival of the English people, there were indigenous people occupying this territory. These people had their own identity, culture, financial, government and legal systems.

However, the invasion of the English and the colonization of the region, resulted in most islands in the Caribbean, being transformed into a replica of England. The English were so powerful that they took away the settlers' way of life - language, culture, norm, food, dress, customs and laws- and replaced them with their own. Until today, numerous practices remain with us despite the declaration of independence. We have been colonized by the English world!

To refresh your memory, I would like you to answer the following questions: Why do Caribbean people believe that they must have a cup of hot beverage as soon as they awake in the morning? Where did that practice originate? Why do you need hot beverage even when the weather is extremely warm?

I will give you the answer; Colonization! The English originally occupied territories which were extremely cold; even freezing at times. To help keep warm they developed the habit of drinking hot beverages at the break of dawn as well as other times during the day.

Let me ask you another question. Where does the idea of wearing three-piece suits in such warm weather conditions originate? If you said, 'Colonization by the English', you would be correct. It was for the same reason which they had hot beverages regularly that they dressed in that manner.

Let's examine our practice in road usage. Why do we drive on the left side of the road? Again, that is how England does it. We have been colonized! The colonized regions also built houses, churches and government buildings, using their architectural designs.

A final example should drive the point home. If you happen to visit a Resident Magistrate or Supreme Court in any of these colonized regions, the attire of the lawyers and judges is a direct result of colonization. There, a judge with dark skin tone may be seen wearing a silver-white peruke (periwig) as well as long black gowns. Get the picture? I believe you have recaptured an image of the effects of the colonization of Caribbean territories by the English. The same scenario is true in regions colonized by the French and the Spanish. However, I did not create that flashback to promote Caribbean History. Instead, I hope it will help you to create a clearer understanding of what God expected to result from Adam's obedience to His command.

Had Adam obeyed God's command before the fall, there would be an even more magnificent display of the splendor of heaven on earth since there would be no evil to contend with. The earth would have been filled with sinless beings, all reflecting the likeness and glory of the unseen God. The first Adam would have fulfilled his purpose and 'colonized the earth'. On earth, God's will would have been done and His kingdom would have come.

Sadly, Adam failed! When he committed that sin - high treason- he surrendered his ambassadorship. He lost his God-given rights and authority to fill the earth with the kingdom of God. The kingdom of darkness immediately took over and eventually colonized the earth.

As you are aware, before Adam sinned, there was nothing called violence in the earth. Peace and contentment were what mankind experienced. There was no poverty; everyone would be wealthy. No one would aspire to rule another individual. Everyone would have everything in common. However, despite Adam's transgression and all the ills that have resulted from the kingdom of darkness seemingly being in power, God's plan for man remains.

Adam's sin led to the infiltration of the kingdom of darkness and opened the door to competitiveness. By the same route entered all the other evil practices which result in the turmoil we presently experience in the earth.

Darkness has engulfed the earth. The message that we are preaching today is the same as the one God gave to Adam. Adam, however, failed to do as he was commanded. Will you fail too? God's plan remains! He is still eager to do what He promised to do from the beginning.

Can you see how the first Adam's transgression messed up his mission? The first son which Adam produced -Cain- was a murderer! Imagine that! God's command was to fill the earth with others like himself and his first offspring was a murderer! Adam failed miserably!

However, God demonstrated His Agape - unconditional- love, and sent another Son with the same mandate which the first Adam failed to accomplish. The last Adam, -Jesus Christ, The Messiah- was given the mandate. Hallelujah! This brought hope again for Adam's fallen race.

Chapter 2

WHY AM I HERE?

The Last Adam

According to the word of God in 1Corinthians 15:45-49 there is a clear distinction between the first and the last Adam.

> *And so, it is written, the first man Adam was made a living soul; the last Adam was made a quickening spirit.*
>
> *Howbeit that was not first which was spiritual, but that which is natural, and afterward that which is spiritual.*
>
> *The first man is of the earth, earthy: the second man is the Lord from heaven.*
>
> *As is the earthy, such are they also that are earthy: and as is the heavenly, such are they also that are heavenly.*

> *And as we have borne the image of the earthy, we shall also bear the image of the heavenly.*

My God from Zion! This is so powerful! It is exciting news for all Christians. Isaiah -the eagle eye Prophet- got a glimpse of Him and revealed His purpose in a clear outline found in Isaiah 9:6

> *For unto us a child is born, unto us a Son is given: and the government shall be upon His shoulder: and His name shall be called Wonderful, Counsellor, The Mighty God, The Everlasting Father, The Prince of Peace.*

You may wonder - What exactly does it mean by:

The government shall be upon His shoulder.

Well – Let me explain! The word 'Government' may be referred to as:

The political direction exercised over the actions of the members, citizens, or inhabitants of communities, societies and states.

There was, therefore, going to be a new leader in this man whose birth was being prophesied or foretold. His purpose or responsibility was to set up a new system of governance. This system was then to be used as the guiding principles to colonize the earth.

This new system would produce a new way of life. Its practices would obliterate or destroy the existing evil system created by the first Adam and his offspring. A new system would be established; a godly and righteous one. The beings of this new system would be indwelt by the quickening Spirit of God. Hallelujah! You and I are most privileged to be recipients of this 'dunamis'. Glory to God!

Under the government of the Messiah, the mandate given in Genesis 1:28 would be ultimately realized! Mankind once again has dominion over all things in the earth. If you are a part of the kingdom of God, this is an awesome time to praise God and declare, I AM UNSTOPPABLE! My God! Hallelujah!

Now, having acknowledged the entrance of the last Adam into the earth realm, we who have accepted Him as our Lord and Saviour, are now joint heirs with Christ. Paul, in Romans 8, so eloquently describes the new creatures which we have become, as well as the benefits to which we are now entitled.

However, we do not escape the responsibilities. Our purpose remains rooted in the instructions which were given to the First Adam. The first instruction was examined in the previous chapter as we focused on the entry and exit of the First Adam. We will continue to establish our purpose from here by focusing on the same instructions but from the perspective of the Last Adam, Jesus Christ.

The second instruction or command given to Adam was to subdue. While the last Adam has equipped, empowered and set the example for us to colonize the earth, we face strong opposition. Hence, believers must remain cognizant of the fact that unclean spirits exist and are constantly lurking around in the earth realm. By no means will the kingdom of darkness accept defeat and surrender to the kingdom of God. Mankind must carry out the instructions God gave - to subdue them all!

Everything which moves on the earth must be kept under man's control. However, before we can put things under our control, we must be fruitful. Note that there is a sequence in the commands; firstly, be fruitful; secondly, subdue or control and thirdly, have dominion. In summary, be a king or a ruler! But fruitfulness is key!

So then, 'What were we called to do?' We were called to do what the first Adam failed to do! I know this has been repeated a few times already. However, I will continue to reiterate it throughout this handbook. Hopefully, by its conclusion, we will all be verbalizing and fulfilling our purpose and mission.

Now since Jesus Christ is the last Adam, let us examine the command which He left for us who presently occupies the earth.

> *St John 15:16*
> *Ye have not chosen me, but I have chosen you, and ordained you, that ye should go and bring forth fruit, and that your fruit should remain: that whatsoever*

ye shall ask of the Father in My name, He may give it you.

This explains why we are in the church. Without this knowledge, our life will be stressful and lead to depression. In the absence of this knowledge, we wander aimlessly; wondering why our lives are going around in circles. If we do not have this awareness, our lives will be meaningless. If we do not know why we are here, our lives will be void of purpose and direction.

I am here to inform those believers who are ignorant and remind those who have forgotten the reason God called everyone into the kingdom. Jesus stated emphatically, "You have not chosen me." I want to emphasize this fact for every believer who is experiencing uncertainty about their position in the kingdom of God.

You did not choose Christ; Christ chose you! You did not choose church; church chose you! I think this is an important point, worthwhile being repeated by every believer reading this handbook. Go ahead and say it, until the message settles in the mind as well as the spirit. Contrary to what many believe, you cannot leave church; but the church most certainly can leave you.

Hello believers! You did not choose Jesus! Jesus chose you! As God, it is impossible for Jesus to lie. These are His words, "You are not the one who chose Me." Do you know why Jesus spoke in such manner? Well, Jesus is the King of all kings; and kings are different from presidents and prime ministers.

Jesus is the King of the kingdom of God. Let me interject here to point out that as Christ's Ambassadors, we do not preach religion. Therefore, whenever you are in the King Jesus Pentecostal Fellowship, of which I am Overseer, you are not in a religious setting. We are members of the Church of the Living God, and as Jesus commanded, we preach the kingdom of God.

The kingdom of God is quite different from religion. You can read more on "religious spirits" in Chapter Two of my book titled Warring Unclean Spirits.

Now, it is imperative that every believer should understand that we did not choose Jesus, but rather He chose us. Jesus' declarations are made from His position as the head of government in the kingdom of God. This system of governance is unlike our political system; not democratic.

In a democratic government or political system, the citizens rule by exercising their power or authority in the decision-making process. The people choose their leader by election. This process allows them to vote in - elect- the person of whom they are in favour and remove the leader of whom they are no longer in favour.

Not so in a kingdom where monarchy is hereditary! Power comes from being born in the royal family. You are not elected by the people to be governed; you are born a king; a ruler. Jesus was not elected by man to be the King, Jesus was born the King!

The king is the one responsible for choosing citizens. Therefore, Jesus could declare, "...I have chosen you." By this we realize that Jesus is establishing a kingdom. In a similar manner to Rome taking over Israel and having it colonized; the kingdom of God is to take over and colonize the kingdom of darkness.

When Rome colonized Israel, their language was changed from Hebrew to Greek. The Roman government's political system replaced the judges, prophets and kings. Their currency was replaced with one bearing the image of Caesar -then governor of Rome-. Roman architecture was now being used to erect buildings. Their food, attire, norms and values were replaced by whatever existed within the Roman culture. Israel had been colonized by Rome!

Jesus brought the kingdom of God to earth. He announced that it was here and commanded those whom He had chosen to become a part of this kingdom, to colonize the world. John the Baptist also made a similar declaration as he prepared the way for King Jesus' entrance into the earth.

> *Matthew 3:1-3*
>
> *In those days came John the Baptist, preaching in the wilderness of Judaea*
>
> *And saying, Repent ye: for the kingdom of heaven is at hand.*
>
> *For this is he that was spoken of by the prophet Esaias, saying, the voice of one*

crying in the wilderness, Prepare ye the way of the Lord, make His paths straight.

The kingdom of God having arrived, would now be evident through the manifestations of the power of God. However, its power would only be noticeable and impacting through colonizing the world and destroying the kingdom of darkness. Whenever someone is chosen by Jesus Christ to be a part of His kingdom, there are tangible evidences of this colonization.

There is a change in the believer's language. Through the baptism of the Holy Ghost, a heavenly language is given to the believer. This language is used in prayer to talk to God. The speech of the believer becomes 'seasoned with salt'; the message of the kingdom of God is on his lips. Every time the believer speaks, the passion with which he declares the good news advances the kingdom of God.

There are visible signs of the take-over by the way believers dress; places they go; things they do with their bodies; how they use their time and resources and the people with whom they associate.

A believer whose life has been over-taken by the Spirit of God, transforms from glory to glory before everyone's eyes. They are not nagged by any church leader about what to wear, where they should no longer go and other trivial matters. The force with which the kingdom of God captures a new believer, produces an unrivalled zeal for the things and presence of God. Only when a believer begins to lose their first love, their focus begins to return to these beggarly elements of the world which they had initially lost appetite for.

> In *Philippians 3:8-14,* the Apostle Paul states: *Yea doubtless, and I count all things but loss for the excellency of the knowledge of Christ Jesus my Lord: for whom I have suffered the loss of all things, and do count them but dung, that I may win Christ,*
>
> *And be found in Him, not having my own righteousness, which is of the law, but that which is through the faith of Christ, the righteousness which is of God by faith:*
>
> *That I may know Him, and the power of His resurrection, and the fellowship of His sufferings, being made conformable unto His death;*
>
> *If by any means I might attain unto the resurrection of the dead.*
>
> *Not as though I had already attained, either were already perfect: but I follow after, if that I may apprehend that for which also, I am apprehended of Christ Jesus.*
>
> *Brethren, I count not myself to have apprehended: but this one thing I do, forgetting those things which are behind, and reaching forth unto those things which are before,*

> *I press toward the mark for the prize of the high calling of God in Christ Jesus.*

Anyone who experiences that kind of take over which Apostle Paul describes, should be able to relate to what I have been saying. Hallelujah! It is similar to what the Prophet Jeremiah described in Jeremiah 20:9

> *Then I said, I will not make mention of Him, nor speak any more in His name. But His word was in mine heart as a burning fire shut up in my bones, and I was weary with forbearing, and I could not stay.*

But! But! But! The kingdom of God coming into the life of a believer, is the real deal! This is not 'like fire' Hallelujah! This is FIRE!!!!!! Glory to God!!!

I know we are looking at the kingdom mandate. But if you have been chosen by God for this great kingdom, I believe you will want to take a moment right now to celebrate with a PRAISE BREAK!!! Hallelujah!!! Glory!!! Thank You Jesus!!! Mighty God of Daniel!!! Glory!!! Hallelujah!!! My God from Zion!!! King of kings!!! Lord of lords!!! JESUS!!! JESUS!!! JESUS!!! PRAISE HIM!!!

I have been colonized! Glory to God! The kingdom of God has taken over my mind, my body, my soul and my spirit. Hallelujah! I have the kingdom walk, the kingdom talk, the kingdom dress; the kingdom culture;

and guess what? I absolutely love it! I love the new, transformed me; the colonized me. I even have a new name, I am a brother in Christ. That's my testimony! What's yours?

You can now fully appreciate and understand why Jesus said, "You have not chosen me, but I have chosen you." No doubt you can recall how deep you were in sin. You will remember that you were not thinking about Him, when He called you. Like Nathanael in St. John 1, you were under your own fig tree, minding your own business, but His eyes were on you.

His eyes were on you and He chose you! Do you know how long ago Jesus made that decision to choose you? From before the foundation of the world! My God from Zion! It sounds unbelievable, but it is true. I wonder if you really know:

Who you are? Whose you are? And Why you are here?

Guess what? The answers to those questions are in fact life-transforming revelations! It is impossible for you to receive this knowledge with a clear understanding of what it means; and not exercise the wisdom that makes your life brand new.

All limits are off whenever you get this! From Adam's time, you were in the plan of God. The first Adam messed up and God pulled back His Spirit from him, but God still did not change His mind about you. He had you in His mind as a logos and released you as a rhema into the earth realm, for such a time as this.

Chapter 3

PURPOSE

The Ministry of Reconciliation

> 2 Corinthians 5:17-20
> *Therefore, if any man be in Christ, he is a new creature: old things are passed away; behold, all things are become new.*
>
> *And all things are of God, who hath reconciled us to Himself by Jesus Christ, and hath given to us the ministry of reconciliation;*
>
> *To wit, that God was in Christ, reconciling the world unto Himself, not imputing their trespasses unto them; and hath committed unto us the word of reconciliation.*
>
> *Now then we are ambassadors for Christ, as though God did beseech you by*

us: we pray you in Christ's stead, be ye reconciled to God.

This powerful portion from God's word not only tells us who we are, or whose we are but also lets us know, why we are here. Now let us look at the reason you were called by Jesus; why He chose you and why you are here.

The Spirit of God summoned me to release the answer to this question of purpose within the body of Christ. All lingering doubts of the believers' purpose should dissipate after reading this.

In revisiting St. John 15 – we will see that verse 16 continues to say:

And ordained you ... Here, 'ordained' may be referred to as:

Make a priest or minister
Confer holy orders on
Appoint, anoint, consecrate

This means that we have been appointed, selected, positioned, set apart, pulled out and placed in the kingdom by Jesus Christ. Even after being made aware of that, the big question remains - 'WHY?'

Finally, Jesus releases the answer,

That you should go and bring forth fruit ...

So, there you have it! You were not chosen to sit within the four walls of the beautiful religious edifice or your comfortable ceiled houses. You were not chosen to 'warm benches', relax, or to 'watch face' -pay attention to others-. Neither were you chosen to watch clothes or focus your attention on who is saying or doing what.

Jesus says, "I chose you that you should GO!" You cannot remain in the same position or place where you first encountered Jesus and answer this call. Jesus sent the lepers to the priests; He sent the man who dwelt among the tombs back to His family; He sent Moses back to Egypt. Where did He send you?

Could it be your workplace, your unsaved relatives and friends, the enemy's camp? Where is He sending you? The good news is that you do not have to be afraid because you are not alone. The Captain of the army of the Lord of Host is with you.

As soon as those who knew you before, see you, they will recognize that there is something different about you. You will begin to show signs of having been with Jesus. They will realize that you are being colonized. That is where trouble begins! But do not fear! You are not alone! The King of the kingdom, along with a host of high-ranking angels is with you. These have been placed on a special assignment to protect you and to wage war against every unclean spirit which attacks your purpose. So, go right ahead and begin to witness to your unsaved family members, co-workers and fellowmen. Go in Jesus name! Be fearless! They too have been chosen to be a part of the kingdom of God.

If you are a member of a congregation that is not going out into the community to witness, something is wrong. A Christian who does not witness is not being obedient to the command of Jesus Christ and is therefore not doing God's work. Do not sit in the church or your ceiled houses. Go into the streets! Get into your community and tell somebody about Jesus.

When was the last time you led someone to Christ? If you do not reach the lost, how are they going to hear the good news and have an opportunity to become a part of the kingdom of God? Don't you know that this is how the church fulfills its mandate? A noticeably disobedient christian is one who sits at home attending to personal affairs, while others are out witnessing.

If you have never got a word to share with somebody; and have never led someone to Christ, you are unfruitful, ungrateful and unfaithful. Jesus said, "I ordain you; I appoint you so that you can GO!" And not just GO! But there is something that is expected to take place as you go. Your impact is supposed to result in your fruitfulness.

GO AND BRING FORTH FRUIT! There you have it! Your purpose clearly stated. Stop reading for a moment. Close your eyes and speak over your life. Declare your purpose until it resonates in the depths of your soul. Come on and declare:

MY PURPOSE IS TO GO AND BRING FORTH FRUIT!

MY PURPOSE IS TO GO AND BRING FORTH FRUIT!

MY PURPOSE IS TO GO AND BRING FORTH FRUIT!
MY PURPOSE IS TO GO AND BRING FORTH FRUIT!
MY PURPOSE IS TO GO AND BRING FORTH FRUIT!
MY PURPOSE IS TO GO AND BRING FORTH FRUIT!
MY PURPOSE IS TO GO AND BRING FORTH FRUIT!

Continue to make this declaration until you are convicted and convinced of your purpose.

It is time for introspection! Ask yourself this question, with a deep consciousness that you are in the presence of a Holy God; from whom nothing is hid:

How much fruit have I borne since I became a part of the kingdom of God?

If there is a fruit tree in your yard and it fails to bear fruit, what would you do with it? It has been watered, pruned, fertilized and nourished in every possible way. However, all it produces are tons of leaves, which you must clean daily; but no fruit. What would you do with that unfruitful tree?

In case you are uncertain, Luke 3:9 answers the question:

And now also the axe is laid unto the root of the trees: every tree therefore which

bringeth not forth good fruit is hewn down and cast into the fire.

Let us go a little further and take an inventory within the body of Christ. This exercise should provoke us to action. When next you are among believers, ask these questions:

> How many fruits have you borne since being born again?
> How many fruits are on your tree?
> Are you fruitful or unfruitful?
> Can you identify anyone within the body of Christ as your fruit?
> Can you irrefutably state that, in keeping with the command of our Lord and Saviour Jesus Christ, you got up, went out and ministered to unsaved and here are the persons who responded to Christ's call, through my witness?

It is imperative for believers to regularly do introspections. The body of Christ as a whole, needs to also take inventories. In the absence of these self-checks, we will become complacent and ineffective in the earth. This ultimately leads to unfruitfulness.

Bear in mind that we do not carry out these exercises to boast of our accomplishments and to expose the unfruitfulness of others. Not at all! That is a wrong motive. Rather we want to rekindle our fire;

renew our zeal and passion for lost souls and ensure God will be pleased with our labour.

Truthfully, a believer without passion for souls is a believer whose life is not being lived with purpose. Having examined ourselves, it is time to move forward in obedience to Jesus' command. God gave us a mandate which makes us aware of our purpose, but that is not all. In fulfilling it, we bring glory and honour to God. Hallelujah!

Now that we can truthfully say that we have been fruitful, what's next? Can we give an account of the fruits that we have borne?

It is commendable to be fruitful; great accomplishment! However, Jesus requires a bit more than that. The measure of fruitfulness in the kingdom of God, extends beyond just bearing fruit to the sustenance and maintenance of the fruit.

So, the question arises, where are the fruits which you have borne? John 15:16 continues:

And that your fruit should remain…

Wow! You mean I am still responsible for these souls even after they are baptized and become members of the church? I think that this responsibility should be for church leaders and officers. Well…According to Jesus, it is yours!

It is therefore not good enough to win others to Christ and then neglect their spiritual growth and development. Your fruit should remain. This means that they will mature in Christ to the point that they themselves begin to bear fruit. This is the means by which the kingdom of God advances forcefully in the realm of the earth. This principle guarantees a great harvest; colonization of the world.

The principle is: Each one Wins One

So, what can I do to have my fruit remain?

I am glad you asked. Here is a list of simple things which you can do:

> Continuing to be a source of encouragement to the new believer;
> Call or send a message to find out how the fruit is progressing;
> Share scriptures and other edifying material;
> Share uplifting songs;
> Pray and fast for the believer and with the believer wherever and whenever possible;
> Refer to your pastor, any matter of concern for the believer which you consider more appropriate for him to address;
> Most importantly, lead by example; be a role model for your fruit.
> Note that the list is by no means inexhaustible.

Like fruitful animals, fruitful people are protective of their fruit. No one wants to face a dog, lion, fowl or any of those mothers from within the animal kingdom that just gave birth. Men and women who parent can identify with those in the animal and bird kingdom, as we too are usually very protective of our young ones. The truth is, in some cases we are over protective and so paranoid that we at times do not realize the appropriate time to let go.

This is equally true in the kingdom of God. You will never want to see someone who you won to Christ struggling or backsliding. If they do, your fruit did not remain.

After the fruit has been snatched from the kingdom of darkness and placed into the kingdom of light, you should be able to watch this fruit transform before your very eyes. According to the system of government established by Jesus Christ, colonization is the process by which the kingdom of God strips the fruit of the nutrients deposited in it by the world and nourishes it with godliness. This nourishment transforms it into the image and likeness of God.

What a beauty to observe our own transformation in words, action, attire and knowledge of the things of God. How mind blowing are the experiences of the tangible manifestations of the power of God! How much more we beam with pride, tempered by humility, when we observe similar transformations in the lives of believers who our witnessing led to Christ. With great joy, like eagles, we soar from glory to glory as the kingdom of God colonizes the earth! Hallelujah!

Glory to God! You are no longer ignorant believers. God sent me to stir you up and I sense in my spirit that your confidence has been restored and so has your zeal to go and do exploits for the Lord. I am sure that you can now boldly declare both your true identity as well as your purpose.

Yes, kingdom citizens! You are Christ's Ambassadors in this earth realm. Your mandate is to bear fruit in order to colonize the earth for Jesus. As each one reaches one, the kingdom of God advances forcefully, and Jesus is glorified.

Before closing this chapter, I would like to address someone specifically. Yes! You are wondering why you are doing the job in which you are currently employed. Why are you operating the business you presently do? I have the answers for you: TO BRING FORTH FRUIT!

Now, ask someone else if you will:

Why did you get that job?

The answer is the same: TO BRING FORTH FRUIT

Each of us is strategically placed in an environment which provides a great opportunity for us to be fruitful. The challenges you face might force you to think otherwise, but it is a lie from the pit of hell. Jesus is saying, "Bloom where you have been planted."

The hidden truth is that beneath the confusion, anxiety, depression and frustration is the absence of a life being lived on purpose. To avoid all these life-threatening emotions, you must endeavor to accomplish the Master's will for your life. Every person who enters your sphere of influence, provides a great opportunity for you to be fruitful. Once you are fruitful, continue to be involved in the life of your fruit so it can remain.

Have you ever wondered why you feel so miserable?

Do you know why you are so depressed?

Why do you think that the devil provides so much work for your hands to do?

Because you are idle! You are unoccupied! Instead of fulfilling your God-given mandate, you are busy engaging in meaningless ventures which makes you unfruitful. Consequences follow unfruitfulness. Some of our bad experiences are therefore self-explanatory.

Unfruitfulness produces powerlessness! I repeat, unfruitfulness produces powerlessness! Anyone who does not witness is powerless. According to the word of God, as the Apostles shared the good news of the kingdom, the Lord God confirmed their words with signs and wonders. If you do not open your mouth and witness, there is nothing for God to accomplish in your life, so you remain unfruitful and powerless.

Having been chosen to colonize the earth, you are expected to colonize your family, your workplace and your community. In fulfilling this mandate, God refers to us as labourers in His vineyard. Now our God is a just God who pays every man according to His deeds- good or evil. Unfruitfulness results in unanswered prayer requests. John 15:16 says that the condition for God to give you that which you ask the Father in His name, is that you be fruitful and that your fruit should remain.

Do you want to be blessed?
Do you want your prayers to be answered?

I guess you know by now what you must get done!

Chapter 4

POWERFUL PRAYERS

This which I am about to say is profound but has been overlooked by many believers. According to the word of God, not witnessing and not nurturing new believers might be the reason for the frustration and discouragement some believers are experiencing.

They keep asking why their prayers go unanswered and their lives appear to be stagnant. However, before you get upset with me, let us look at the latter part of the verse we have been most recently dissecting in this handbook.

John 15:16
THAT WHATSOEVER YE SHALL ASK OF THE FATHER IN MY NAME, HE MAY GIVE IT YOU.

Well! There you have it! So, while receiving from God has not been the motivation behind being fruitful, it is a rich benefit for which we are indeed grateful. Having been fruitful and having a spirit which nurtures the fruit that it should remain, Jesus now announces that we have acquired a guarantee that the Lord will grant our requests made to Him. Hallelujah! That's awesome!

Let me share with you what God has said to me. He said: Son, notice - dominion and the power to subdue is a sequence; an order. This first comes through witnessing or bringing forth fruit.

Do you remember that God's first instruction was "BE FRUITFUL?" After being fruitful, you receive the anointing- the authority, 'exusia' to subdue. Pay attention to this illustration: I walk into a house which has ten witchcraft demons. My mission on entering is to bring forth fruit. As I begin to speak the good news of the kingdom of God, these occupants begin to open their spirits to receive Jesus as their Lord and Saviour.

Why? Because we belong to Jesus and carry the kingdom of God within us. My entrance into that or any other environment subdues and brings under subjection every demon by the power of God in us as believers.

Without this power, you will be praying for hours in a house and the demons remain in control of the persons whom you are trying to win to Christ. This explains why some believers are in workplaces controlled by the powers of darkness and these unclean spirits are not brought under subjection. Believers, we cannot afford to have a form of godliness and deny its power.

I guess I should elaborate more on why even some believers who are filled with the Holy Spirit are powerless and unfruitful, even in their homes. If you are not fulfilling the first command which God gave to mankind, the power of God has no opportunity to manifest in your life, confirming the message of the kingdom which you need to share.

At whatever point in your life you begin to bring forth fruit, God promises to perform that which you ask Him to do. He has an unbroken record in His faithfulness! Hallelujah! Success is guaranteed whenever the believer presents himself at any location to deliver souls with the leading of the Holy Spirit.

Chapter 5

ACTION TIME

The Great Commission

Whenever you begin to pull people into the church, as you open your mouth, regardless of the number or nature of demons present, they must be subjected to the Spirit of Jesus Christ within you because you have power to subdue them. They must be subdued!

Only those who obey the first command goes on to experience the second. Conclusively, the persons who become kings in the earth; having dominion over the earth and its resources are those who learn how to bring forth fruit. They begin to exercise the authority to subdue every spirit which opposes them.

The problem within the body of Christ is that we need more persons who know their purpose and begin to walk in their purpose. Do you remember what your purpose is? Yes! To bring forth fruit. Make sure you continue to repeat it until it resonates in your spirit. That way, long after you have closed this handbook, you do not walk away forgetting your purpose.

Without purpose, life will be meaningless, and one will become barren; unfruitful; and good for nothing. God has no use for these kinds of persons. It is equally important to know your purpose and to walk in it.

Jesus' final words remains His most important utterances. That holds true for anyone. One can speak a million different things during his lifetime and make a million promises. Upon that person's passing, his final instructions, especially if they are documented and endorsed by his signature, supersedes everything previously spoken.

Within the legal system it is referred to as the person's 'Last Will and Testament'. A man's final words therefore are his most important words. Do you want to know what Jesus' most important words were? Let's take a look at them. They were spoken just before He ascended into heaven.

Jesus said in St. Matthew 28:

> *All power is given unto me in heaven and in earth.*
>
> *Go ye therefore, and teach all nations, baptizing them in the name of the Father, and of the Son, and of the Holy Ghost.*

Go! Go! Go! Were Jesus' final words.

Time to go!
Time to go!
You had better go!
You must go!

Go! Jesus said, preach and baptize. This is equivalent to Him saying, "Go and bring forth fruit."

The question today is:

How many believers have received those words and are obeying them?

Jesus says to tell you that if you refuse to go, He will step over you and find someone else. It could be your father, mother, cousin, children, aunt, uncle or siblings. He might find a scammer, prostitute, gunman or someone else who you view as nobody or nothing. He will save them and send them to do what you were initially called to do.

Jesus told the church that if they refused to carry out the mandate, He would raise up sticks and stones to get it done. What is He referring to when He says, "sticks and stones?" He is referring to Gentiles. That's us! The people who weren't Israelites; as the Israelites were considered the Olive Tree.

Jesus is so powerful, He is not dependent on any individual to carry out His mandate. When Jesus made reference to 'sticks', He was referring to those who are out of covenant, those who have been separated from Him; those who were broken off and are dry. These He would have engrafted to the Olive Tree and use to do the work of bringing others into the kingdom.

Who do you think 'stones' are? The hardened, tough hearted persons! The ones who have no feelings; like some murderers and killers who have no live conscience. Men who are not afraid to take the lives of others in gruesome ways and walk away smiling. They are so heartless that they go on to boast and party about the murders which they commit.

God is saying to those who are sitting at ease in the church; those who refuse to go and win souls for the kingdom: Well! If you do not kill, fornicate and steal but are reluctant to do my work; will not fulfil your purpose; I will step over you. I will choose a killer; I will convict him; I will convert him; I will fill him with the Holy Ghost and fire and commission him to go.

I will send him to subdue the very spirits which once held him captive and to set others free. Be reminded that in the past, God used the donkey, the john crow, the raven and those who were considered 'nobodies' to have His mission accomplished.

If you continue to sit in the church comfortably and 'warm the benches' (be idle), God has an alternate plan to ensure that the gospel of the kingdom goes into all the earth. Yes! He will raise up wood and stones because His work must be done!

This earth must be colonized by the kingdom of God. God wants to take control of some peoples' lives, fill them with 'dunamis' power and use them to let the world know that the kingdom of God is here!

Do you know the signs that the kingdom of God is here? According to Matthew 10:7-8, they are:

1. The Gospel preached
2. Sick healed
3. Dead raised
4. Demons cast out
5. Lepers cleansed

Wherever the kingdom of God is, manifestation of God's power takes place. Are you willing to declare that the kingdom of God MUST flow through you? Are you determined that the kingdom of God MUST manifest through you? If you are, go ahead and make those declarations over your life.

THE KINGDOM OF GOD MUST MANIFEST THROUGH ME!

Repeat for emphasis and continue to declare it until you feel the power of Almighty God, rising in your spirit, giving you confidence that you can now 'go' and be fruitful.

The kingdom of God must manifest through me! Utter it until you feel it in the depths of your being. Demons must tremble whenever your name is called. Whenever you show up under the anointing and in the power of the Holy Ghost, demons must flee. Their wings must be broken through the power of God at work in you.

As you engage the kingdom of darkness, unclean spirits must be immobilized in Jesus' name! Demons must be subdued and brought into subjection. Hallelujah! They must return to the kingdom of darkness with reports of defeat because as you open your mouth, the fire of God begins to burn them.

I trust that you really have the knowledge and revelation that whenever the kingdom of God impacts your life, demons are able to identify you as a threat to the kingdom of darkness. In Acts 19, an interesting incident was documented involving the sons of Sceva and the exorcists, vagabond Jews. Can you recall what the demons asked those imposters who sought to expel them in the name of Jesus?

Verse 15 says: ***And the evil spirit answered and said, Jesus I know, and Paul I know; but who are ye?***

Did you hear that? I know about Jesus! I know about Paul! I have encountered them, and they dealt with us wickedly; but who are you? Whenever the kingdom of God takes you over, its impact on your life makes you a threat to the kingdom of darkness. You become the devil's worst nightmare! Demons get instant headaches whenever you enter a house.

The unclean spirits scream for you not to enter that house. You see, they know that once you do, they must leave. Mighty God! Whenever you set foot in that house, somebody's life will be changed! If it is a business place, as soon as you enter, things will turn upside-down.

**I wonder if anyone is stirred up and ready to say:
God here I am
Lord make me a soul winner!
Is anyone crying, Lord send me into homes?
Is anyone pleading, Lord send me into communities?**

I guarantee that anywhere you go and talk about the kingdom of God, those to whom you are ministering will be moved to tears. I can also guarantee that at the end of your witnessing, someone is going to ask for prayer. Someone will be touched, and lives will be transformed when Jesus is presented to them. The message of the kingdom causes lives to change!

Who doesn't want to be a part of this great mission?

Come on believers! Do you have that determination to fulfill your purpose? Paul spoke of stars in our crowns; how many are in yours? He saw each soul won for the Lord as a star. You know that stars give light. Each person who is converted as a result of your witnessing becomes a star in your crown. That believer in turn becomes a light, shining in darkness. Each soul won for the kingdom of God goes back to their environment to illuminate it. They begin to wreak havoc on the kingdom of darkness. In the process they eventually become soul winners too.

Are there any stars in your crown?

I want you to note that the stars in your crown are the enemy's worst nightmare! As a result, they are targeted by the devil. So, your work does not end even after they have come into the kingdom and begin to win souls. On the contrary, the battle intensifies! Are you tenacious enough to continue to engage the forces of darkness so that your labour be not in vain?

If so, declare:

I know my purpose and I am going to fulfil it!

Yes! Declare that the souls which you have won for the kingdom of God, will remain! Hallelujah! If you win one soul for Jesus, ensure you do all that is possible for him to continue to abide in the faith. In retrospect, can you account for the souls which you led to the Lord?

If they are still abiding in the faith, you have great reason to lift your hands in praise and worship! That is awesome! If not, what are you going to do about it? Being serious about soul winning requires making these bold declarations: I am going to turn this world up-side-down! I am going to win the lost at any cost! My fruit shall remain in Jesus' name!

Followed by these declarations, must be an unrelenting tenacity to go! Many start out with such great zeal to win the lost, but in the end, they are won over by the devil instead. The bible states in:

> *Proverbs 11:30:*
> *The fruit of the righteous is a tree of life; and he that winneth souls is wise.*

This statement would suggest that there are strategies involved in soul winning; and in fact, there are! Being effective in this area of ministry requires having knowledge of these strategies and observing them. This demonstration of wisdom will result in the believer influencing the sinner and not the reverse. So Christian youths will not be fearful that instead of converting their unsaved classmates, they will be influenced into cursing, swearing and other unholy and ungodly practices. We have confidence; as John writes in:

> *1John 4:4:*
> *Ye are of God, little children, and have overcome them: because greater is He that is in you, than He that is in the world.*

One of the most important things to remember, is that you are not out there to draw people to yourself.

Lead them to Christ!

Contrary to popular belief, the kingdom of God is far more powerful than the kingdom of darkness. Believers should therefore be resolute that the kingdom of darkness will not be allowed to steal them from the kingdom of God. We have power!

> *But ye shall receive power, after that the Holy Ghost is come upon you: and ye shall be witnesses unto me both in Jerusalem, and in all Judaea, and in Samaria, and unto the uttermost part of the earth. Acts 1:8*

Jesus says that after the Holy Ghost is come upon a believer, he receives power! This is a quickening power; which means we become alive. We do not only receive power, but we become His witnesses. By interpretation, we become duplicates of Jesus!

This duplication makes us a threat to the kingdom of darkness. When the devil sees an empowered witness, he is seeing a reminder of Jesus. This explains why Peter, Paul and all those who received the resurrection power, wreaked havoc on unclean spirits.

The pioneers of the early church, full of the power of the Holy Ghost, not only impacted the kingdom of God by colonizing their world but also placed a huge dent in the kingdom of darkness. They led many to believe on our Lord and Saviour, Jesus Christ. As they preached, signs and wonders confirmed their words.

They were very fruitful in the kingdom of God and went on to record the inspired scriptures, which we now study to show ourselves approved unto God. There are a few men who graced the earth with their presence and left such an astounding impact that both heaven and hell note their accomplishments.

Anyone shares a similar desire? Is anyone determined to be used by God in such a supernatural way that even hell must record your impact on its kingdom?

For me, it's all or nothing!
How about you?

Hell must document my presence in this earth! At my passing, hell must have a 'ball' and hope that no one else dares to create the impact which I created or better yet, exceed it!

My aim is to be so potent in the power of the Holy Ghost, that like Elisha my very bones are full of resurrection power! In that way, even after I have exited this stage of life, I continue to impact lives and cause transformation. Glory to God! I feel like praising Him, who was, and is and is to come. Anyone else wants to outdo those who were so valiant before us?

We are right in the centre of Jesus' will, if we have such desires. In John 14:12, Jesus says:

> *Verily, verily, I say unto you, He that*
> *believeth on me, the works that I do shall*

he do also; and greater works than these shall he do, because I go unto My Father.

Wow! What a promise! Lord let Your will be done in me.

It is my prayer and earnest desire that as long as I am alive, the earth will see tangible manifestations of the power of God in this little lump of clay. Everywhere I go, lives must be transformed! Healing, deliverance, salvation, resurrection and blessings must be supernaturally released by the power of God at work in me. People must serve God because I dare to defy all satanic host and introduce them to the all-powerful God, Jesus Christ.

Anybody else willing to declare in like manner:

Lord I have determined that I will not die but live and declare Your works!
Lord I will fulfil my purpose!
Lord I will not leave behind an unfinished task!

If I were created to have a thousand stars in my crown, I flatly refuse to settle for nine hundred and ninety-nine. I have resolved in my heart that wherever I go, I am going to talk about God! Wherever I go, I am going to preach the kingdom message! People do not need a religion, they need the kingdom of God. That informs my message! That allows me to know what to preach.

Witnessing is a must!
Witnessing is a must!
Bearing fruit is a must!
Bearing fruit is a must!

If you do not witness, you are not fulfilling your God-given mandate; you are not fulfilling your purpose. Remember Jesus' last words were, **"Go and witness!"**

Chapter 6

READINESS TIPS

Having established why we are here as believers, let us move on to the art of witnessing. This includes strategies for witnessing, preparation for witnessing and the process involved in witnessing.

I must interject here to remind you that colonization is a process; and process involves time. While we are growing and changing from glory to glory, there will still be noticeable signs that we have come out of Egypt, but God is still transforming us, to get Egypt out of us.

Each believer will also be at a different stage in the process of being colonized. This requires love, patience and tolerance towards each other. It is important to bear in mind also that some aspects of the transformation require financial support. This involves making some lifestyle, habitual and attire changes.

While we bear these in mind, the zeal to go and be fruitful should not be suppressed in a believer who is in transition. Instead, with the leading of the Holy Ghost and application of wisdom for winning souls, we should observe the following tips.

Attire

These are a few practical tips which should be considered as a kingdom citizen prepares to go into the kingdom of darkness to witness. Within the context of varying cultures, believers should be appropriately attired, especially, when going out to represent your local church body and Jesus Christ.

Females are usually more likely to be in breach of modesty in dress. However, as fashion trends in men's clothing increase, more and more men too are having difficulties in establishing what is appropriate attire, as a child of God.

It would be helpful to be uniformed in attire to avoid these pitfalls. Printed shirts, bearing church logos and themes are quite useful. However, whatever is being worn, seductive and sexually appealing clothing must be avoided. These include those that are too fitted or too revealing.

There is a trend in Christendom among women where the skirts and dresses are rather long but are very tight! This is a No! No! Kingdom minded persons do not create any conscious distractions while witnessing. More importantly, the mandate is to draw people to Christ; not to ourselves.

If we are witnessing to someone and their focus is on us and not the message we are presenting, it is important for us to do a self-check. We need to find out if they are reacting to the manner in which we have presented ourselves.

Modesty should characterize the appearance of believers. It is difficult to explain what modesty will look like in each culture; but thank God for the power of the Holy Spirit who leads us into all truth. A Spirit filled believer is never comfortable in immodesty! This is one of the inexplicable ways that a leader is able to watch the life transforming power of God on display in a believer's life. It is one of the ways growth and maturity in Christ is seen, without the interference of church leaders.

This garment of modesty comes out of a spirit that is fully submitted to God and is anchored in humility. This is the universal clothing for kingdom citizens across the globe and in every culture. When this is seen in the realm of the spirit, it is very easily recognized and admired. This releases church leaders from the burden of detailing what believers should or should not wear.

The plan of the enemy is to use these trivial matters to distract and divide the church. He will also use it to discourage others who are less privileged. On the other hand, he uses it to fill more fortunate believers with pompous pride.

Let us bear in mind that we are witnesses. We are Ambassadors for Christ and as such we should always be in a state of readiness to represent Jesus and to present the gospel to a lost and dying world. The way we attire speaks volumes and should therefore be in adherence to the guidelines of your local church and more importantly, the Spirit of God. Witnessing should never be seen as a local church campaign to get new members. IT IS SPIRITUAL WARFARE!

As you prepare yourself to go witnessing, be careful to follow your leader's command as they follow Christ. Disobedience opens doors to unclean spirits which lessens or even nullifies your impact on the kingdom of darkness. If while you are in the church, your dressing blocks you from being fruitful, it is a clear indication that the spirit of the world still holds you in captivity. You need to be delivered so that God can use you to deliver others.

There is a kingdom dressing! Is that news to you? Well, Yes! There is peculiar way the saints of God present themselves, that makes them identifiable in any crowd. Whenever kingdom sisters are appropriately dressed, kingdom brothers do not undress them; nor vice versa. Undressing takes place both mentally and physically. According to the word of God, lust takes places within the mind before any utterance or action reveals the intents of one's heart.

I am not ignorant of the fact that there are some new believers who are still on the Potter's wheel in that area of their life. God given wisdom must be exercised in dealing with these diverse situations; while ensuring that the zeal for the Lord of Hosts is not suppressed in the lives of these babes in Christ.

Suffice to say, in whatever culture, the children of God are required to be different from the world in their attire. It is important to observe the guidelines established by the leader God has set over your local church. *Obedience is better than sacrifice.*

Oneness in the body of Christ is materialized when we have all things in common. This also includes our manner of dress. God requires that it be modest.

Finally! Whatever you are sold out to, will colonize you. The apostles were called 'Christians' in Antioch. Their unity in attire and manner of life, informed their world that they were different. They looked like Christ! Clearly, they were in the world but not of the world.

Being colonized by the kingdom of God makes us so unified in our appearance that the enemies cannot even tell us apart. When they sought Jesus to crucify Him, it took Judas to point Him out with a kiss of betrayal. They all appeared as one!

Don't be misled! I am not advocating for church folks to wear uniforms everywhere they go. No! I am addressing the impact that modesty in dressing has on the kingdom of darkness. Undoubtedly, it is one of the distinguishing factors, separating the citizens of the kingdom of darkness from those of the kingdom of light. It is an obvious statement that 'we are different'!

In general, it is appropriate for kingdom sisters to wear their clothes below their knees and properly cover all private and sexually appealing body parts. Kingdom brothers on the other hand, should not wear their pants with waists falling to their knees.

Whether witnessing as an organized group or not, the same principles should be observed. In fact, we are always Christ's Ambassadors and therefore represent Him.

It is commonly noted in the body of Christ that single believers who desire to be married, aspire for the best from the opposite sex. Be reminded that you are expected to represent your companion in all areas, including your attire. No kingdom man would want to marry a sister whose tendency is to expose areas of her body. Some things are meant to be reserved for his eyes only, in holy matrimony.

Likewise, no kingdom sister would be attracted to a brother whose pants is well below his waist and so tight that one cannot readily distinguish him from an unbeliever. What is the point of all this? There is a kingdom attire! If you are a part of God's kingdom, wear it! Your conformity is an indication of your submissiveness to the Holy Spirit and your local church leadership. This is honourable in God's sight!

Hygiene

In preparation for witnessing, good hygiene practices must be observed. However, since we are constantly engaging in conversation during witnessing, it is wise to ensure our breath remains fresh. You can travel with a little mouthwash or breath-freshener and use as needed.

Another important hygiene factor is body odour. Taking regular baths, using a deodorant and body fragrance, cologne or perfumes are perfect for eliminating unpleasant odours. Clean clothes also reduce bad odours.

Remember that throughout the scriptures, cleanliness is required by God. Surely it was not only with reference to the spirit but also the flesh.

Witnessing is warfare! It requires readiness; readiness is not just spiritual in nature but also physical and mental. To be effective, you must be prepared. You will not be able to attract anyone to the kingdom of God, whose appearance is worldly, yet yours bear resemblance to theirs. You will not be able to share the gospel without distractions, if you are not modest. But pay attention also to hygiene because you will repel those with whom you want to share the Good News, if your hygiene practices are poor.

GET READY!
IT'S TIME TO SHARE THE GOOD NEWS!

Chapter 7

THE GOOD NEWS

The message of the kingdom; the Gospel of Jesus Christ; the Good News is what Ambassadors for Christ share as they embark on witnessing. However, effective witnessing requires preparation.

> *Study to shew thyself approved unto God, a workman that needeth not to be ashamed, rightly dividing the word of truth.* 2 Timothy 2:15

Know what to say to unbelievers! You should never approach people with arguments about the following:
Which church is right or wrong
Which is the right or wrong day for worship
What should be eaten or not eaten
What should be worn or not worn
Which baptism is right or wrong
Who is going to hell or heaven

No! No! No! That is not the message of the kingdom!

Jesus gave us the kingdom message to take to the world and that is what He wants us to present to them.

What Is the Kingdom Message?

The Kingdom Message is the Good News of the power of God at work in the earth through believers. Here are a few of the things included in the kingdom message:

What God can do
What God has done
What God has done in your life
What you witnessed that God has done in the lives of others
God can deliver
God can heal
God can save
God can provide
God can raise the dead
The power of God is available to deliver anyone from any situation in which s/he finds him/herself.

God is the King of the kingdom to which you belong. Let them know what you have seen King Jesus do.

Avoid all doctrinal debates and conflict over words. A very common debate begins from the declaration that

'JESUS IS GOD!' It is the truth! But that is not the kingdom message. The enemy will be more than happy to use it to start a debate. If he is allowed to have his way, you will eventually waste hours of precious soul winning time engaging in a useless debate.

According to scripture the truth that 'Jesus is God' cannot be taught, but rather it can only be revealed! Once someone gets this revelation, there is an instant transformation in that individual's life! You will recall also, that it was not that message which convicted you to accept Jesus Christ as your Lord and Saviour.

The devil gets excited whenever we engage in conversations which will divert unbelievers from hearing about the power of God on display. He has fooled many into believing that he is in total control and that God has failed to do what He said He would do in these last days. To be a living testimony to the fact that the devil is lying about that, makes you armed and dangerous! You are the devil's worst nightmare!

You are God's witnesses that He is the same yesterday, today and forever! If the devil cannot kill you, he is surely going to try to shut you up! He will stop at nothing to hinder you from going to witness. If he cannot shut you up and he cannot hinder you from going to witness, his next option will be to create distractions or have you bring the wrong message.

Remember now!

He that winneth souls is wise Proverbs 11:30.

Here is a wisdom key: You cannot scale the fish before you catch it! How can you want to scale a fish that you have not even yet caught? Be wise! You must first catch the fish and then you can eventually scale it.

Here is another wisdom key: do not try to scale the fish while it is still alive and in the boat; especially if the boat is still on the water. If you act so foolishly, the fish might get away from your hold and end up in its original position - the water. There is no guarantee that you will catch that fish again.

Here is yet another wisdom key: take the fish to dry land and then begin to prepare it. The best time is when it is lifeless.

These are parables which the wise soul winner should understand. However, if you are uncertain, this is in essence what I am saying: Do not engage in certain conversations with unbelievers. These include those aforementioned and any other that will do more harm than good in leading an unbeliever to Christ.

Whenever you go on the battlefield, your only aim should be to present the message of the kingdom of God. Your only desire should be to see the world come to know Christ as the King of kings and Lord of lords. The world therefore needs to hear that God is here to deliver; to set them free!

Hell cannot refute that message! The power in this 'rope of hope' cannot be neutralized! Demons cannot defeat this message! When the good news is delivered under the anointing and unction of the Holy Ghost, it is so potent! Everything in its way have to yield, as it propels its way into the unbelievers' belly as a quick, sharp two-edged sword.

The very fiber of the soul receiving this message is stirred to know that God is ALL POWERFUL! This creates a hunger and thirst for the kingdom of God. That is what this dying world needs! The world is groaning, eagerly anticipating the manifestation of God's power in the earth realm.

If the message of Jesus and His kingdom has been accepted when you would have presented it, then the search is over. The kingdom is that pearl for which the world intensely searches. It is that lost treasure for which they seek. You found it when you accepted the message of the kingdom and they will too!

How to Win Souls

Tell unbelievers about the kingdom of God. In the process, your gifts will begin to manifest. Yes! As you engage in fulfilling your God-given mandate, your gifts begin to be unwrapped. Actually, that's the exact reason you are gifted, to colonize the earth by allowing the power of God to be manifested; your gifts on display!

Chapter 8

ALTAR WORKERS

Do you feel called to this area of ministry?
Do you possess a strong desire to position yourself at the altar to work for the Lord?

If you do not have that desire as a believer, something is wrong with you. Once you have a passion for lost souls, there will always be an urge to go to someone at the altar. There should be a yearning to participate in the service of winning the lost at any cost. An altar worker's role is pivotal in bringing souls into the kingdom of God.

It should be understood that every unsaved who walks to an altar, has at least one demon within him or her. Did you get that? So, whenever an unsaved walks to the altar, they are not taking that journey by themselves. Demonic spirits accompany them.

Warning! The altar is a WAR ZONE!

This warning goes especially to parents who allow their children to play at the altar. You need to realize that you are putting your children at serious risk and in deadly danger. Parents should cease and desist this practice immediately! It is extremely dangerous and must not be allowed!

Sometimes when the behaviour of some of these children is observed, one cannot help but wonder if some of those demons which were cast out at the altar, have possessed them. Some time ago, during a night service, while I was praying for a woman at the altar, the Lord revealed to me that she had forty-nine demons. While I was praying for her, all forty-nine told me their names. Do not be fooled, some persons coming to the altar are possessed with three hundred or more demons. Some persons have a thousand or more demons living inside them. The bible mentioned a man who had four thousand unclean spirits indwelling him. Can you imagine that! Those demons empowered him to the point where he broke even the chains which were used to restrain him. My God!

The anointing at the altar makes it the only place that God can deliver some of these persons from these demons. The altar cannot therefore be scantly regarded or taken lightly. It is a serious place! When the bible says that the house of God is a dreadful place, what do you think makes it dreadful? The altar of course!

The altar of God is indeed a dreadful place. Whenever you go to the altar therefore, you need to be careful. It is not a place to show-off yourself or to act powerful. As the prayers and praises go up to God in the third heaven, the anointing of God begins to come down. Demons are unable to remain in this supercharged atmosphere. They become restless and begin to manifest. In the process they are being expelled from the persons which they indwell.

However, they cannot function without a body and so they begin a desperate search for someone else to indwell. You will not receive these teachings in an ordinary church setting, so I must share it with you through this medium. I am not trying to scare you, but it is important for you to understand what you are up against on the battlefield as warriors. This information can reduce the number of casualties.

So then, you might ask:

If I am desirous of ministering to someone who has walked to the altar, what must I do?

Firstly, be aware that the person to whom you desire to minister, is possessed with at least one unclean spirit. The responsibility of unclean spirits during this moment will be to hinder unbelievers from becoming christians. The demon assigned to each unbeliever declares that the person is his house. Before I go any further, I think there is the need to point out some things about demons from the scriptures.

Luke 11:18-26 provides some important information.

If Satan also be divided against himself, how shall his kingdom stand? Because ye say that I cast out devils through Beelzebub.

And if I by Beelzebub cast out devils, by whom do your sons cast them out? Therefore, shall they be your judges.

But if I with the finger of God cast out devils, no doubt the kingdom of God is come upon you.

When a strong man armed keepeth his palace, his goods are in peace:

But when a stronger than he shall come upon him, and overcome him, he taketh from him all his armour wherein he trusted, and divideth his spoils.

He that is not with me is against me: and he that gathereth not with me scattereth.

When the unclean spirit is gone out of a man, he walketh through dry places, seeking rest, and finding none, he saith, I will return unto my house whence I came out.

And when he cometh, he findeth it swept and garnished.

Then goeth he, and taketh to him seven other spirits more wicked than himself; and they enter in, and dwell there: and the last state of that man is worse than the first.

We are reminded in the word of God that we do not fight against each other as human beings. Instead, we fight against unclean spirits which have their dwelling inside human beings. This includes principalities which function in a similar manner as school principals do; they give out orders.

Next in rank are powers; these carry out great and mighty destructive acts. These are responsible for some accidents, hurricanes, tsunamis, tornados and other atrocities which cannot be explained naturally.

Then there are rulers of darkness of this world. These are unclean spirits which rule different territories. Below these are spiritual wickedness in high places, these dwell in the atmosphere and there are others which make their abode or dwelling inside human beings.

Ephesians 6:12
For we wrestle not against flesh and blood, but against principalities, against powers, against the rulers of the darkness of this world, against spiritual wickedness in high places.

There are demons which are positioned at specific geographical locations. Some demons reside in grave yards; some dwell in the waters; some are stationed at crossroads. Accident demons are dispatched on highways. This explains why there are some areas on our roadways which are prone to accidents. I do hope someone is being enlightened about the works of darkness which we engage in warfare.

All those desirous of working at the altar needs to be knowledgeable of the things being highlighted at this juncture. These are tools to make you wiser and to increase your effectiveness as an altar worker.

Be warned! Altar workers, you must learn how to operate in this atmosphere!

According to the scriptures, there are two kingdoms- the satanic kingdom and God's kingdom. God's kingdom casts out devils. Jesus was doing exactly that when He encountered opposition from the religious leaders. Their explanation of the miracle was that Jesus was using satanic powers -Beelzebub- to cast out the demons. Jesus, in refuting their claim, pointed out something which is so profound that no Christian warrior should forget.

SATAN DOES NOT FIGHT AGAINST HIMSELF!

The finger of God in the scriptures refers to the power of God. Whenever demons are cast out of persons, the kingdom of God is come upon them. The anointing of God on the person provides the power which the enemy cannot withstand. The demons therefore must go! Hallelujah!

Psalm 97:1-5 declares this about the atmosphere filled with the presence, Spirit and power of God:

> *The Lord reigneth; let the earth rejoice; let the multitude of isles be glad thereof.*
>
> *Clouds and darkness are round about Him: righteousness and judgment are the habitation of His throne.*
>
> *A fire goeth before Him and burneth up His enemies round about.*
>
> *His lightnings enlightened the world: the earth saw, and trembled.*
>
> *The hills melted like wax at the presence of the Lord, at the presence of the Lord of the whole earth.*

Unclean spirits melts in the presence of the Spirit of God in a similar fashion as wax melts in the presence of fire. In other words, demons melt whenever the kingdom of God - the manifest power of God is present.

The human body is referred to as the house in which unclean spirits dwell. Whenever the Spirit of God comes upon a man, the unclean spirits are cast out of his body –the house. The kingdom of God then takes over that body and indwells that human being.

If a person is not on the Lord's side, they are automatically on the devil's side. There is no middle ground. It is therefore very easy to identify which kingdom the people who fight against the church belong; as it is impossible for an individual to be on God's side -indwelt by the Spirit of God- and oppose the works of God!

The demons which are cast out of a man delivered by God, do not die. Spirits cannot die! Instead they go about in search of another house – another body into which they can take up residence. You might recall that human bodies are a necessity for them to function in the earth realm.

A serious problem develops whenever these unclean spirits enter someone else. Remember I told you that everyone has their own demons which have been assigned to them. This happens in some instances at birth. These unclean spirits consider the human beings they indwell, their personal property. When an unclean spirit which was cast out of someone else seeks residence in another person, they become squatters in another unclean spirit's territory.

This make them subordinate to the demons which were there initially. Instead of being in control in this human being, they are being treated as slaves; being given orders to carry out. This renders it impossible for them to find peace in this house. Demons which were expelled from a human body, lose their rank in the kingdom of darkness for allowing themselves to be evicted from their houses.

This inability to find rest stirs a desire to go back to their original house where they would be in ultimate control. As you observed in the aforementioned scripture, the demon referred to the human body in which he dwelt as his own house. There he is ruler and controller; he gives the orders which must be carried out by other spirits subordinate to him in this person's life. Here the real danger begins!

The unclean spirit is adamant that it must control and indwell that person until death! If you examine the scriptures keenly, you will learn that demons speak. Demons move; they have the ability to travel to anywhere in the earth realm which they desire. Demons can go in and out of human beings. Demons can get tired. They can feel pain. Demons can get weary; unable to find any rest. They are able to see. They can hear. They are able to conspire. They plan; they know that they possess varying strengths and abilities. The wisdom of the serpent inspires that demon which was cast out of his original house, before reentering, to seek out and conspire with seven additional demons. Take note of the description of those demons which he recruited. They were more wicked than himself. Wow! This was a strategic move to ensure that there is little or no chance of eviction again.

Altar workers' pay attention to the nature and characteristics of the enemies you are engaging in spiritual warfare. You need therefore, to carefully and prayerfully approach the altar to minister. I hope you are taking note!

Demons are real beings!

They are not physical, but they are real! They can and will cause havoc in the lives of people.

The plan of the unclean spirits at work in the lives of unsaved persons at the altar is to hinder them from water baptism. They know that as soon as someone is baptized, he enters a covenant with God. This person's body now belongs to Jesus Christ because it was purchased with the blood of Jesus Christ. This strip the demons of their legal rights to this person's body.

Warning! Christians MUST NOT cast demons out of an unsaved person. I will repeat: Christians MUST NOT cast demons out of unsaved persons. This is strange news for some. I can see you in the realm of the spirit, looking puzzled and asking **WHY?**

The bible describes someone out of whom the demon was cast, as a clean, empty house. This emptiness signifies the absence of the Spirit of God which indwells the soul which is surrendered to Jesus Christ. So, if the demon is expelled but the person refuses to give his life to Jesus, that house is open to reentry by that demon.

However, he first solicits help and form an alliance with seven demons more wicked than himself and together they repossess the unsaved. This is detrimental to the person because this regimented force is relentless in their efforts to remain in control of the individual's life. This person's latter position would now be far worse than before.

Therefore, your primary responsibility is to lead the unsaved person to accept Jesus Christ as their personal

Lord and Saviour. Once they have received Him and are in covenant with Him, it is safe to cast out the unclean spirits because the person is now a believer. This guarantees comprehensive coverage under the powerful blood of Jesus Christ. All demons occupying new believers' lives become trespassers because they are now bought with a price - the precious blood of Jesus.

Each new believer belongs to Jesus. This makes it so much easier for the demon to be cast out. I recall one incident in which a young lady decided to give her life to Christ. Immediately, the head demon controlling her life, audibly proclaimed that she cannot take on the name of Jesus because she belongs to him. His voice was horrible as he threatened that she dared not step into the baptismal pool. I silenced him in the name of Jesus, asked her name and enquired whether she wanted to accept Jesus. She said "Yes!" I instructed the baptizer to baptize her in the name of Jesus Christ and then take her back to the service for deliverance.

When she came back from the pool, the demon began to manifest once more; this time, threatening to kill her and insisting that he would not be leaving her body. I stood in my Apostolic anointing; called for the consecrated olive oil; poured it down her throat and released the fire of God on that devil. He came out screaming, leaving the new believer weak and lifeless for a while. She was now free to live for Jesus because she was both saved and delivered.

As a believer, there are times when unclean spirits want to keep you in bondage. All you need to do is to begin to worship God and they have to leave. Remember that once you belong to Jesus, they are trespassers!

Unclean spirits have no legal rights in believers.

We are purchased with the blood of Jesus. We are REDEEMED! Hallelujah!

I do not want you to miss the point I am making. Every unsaved who comes to the altar is possessed by an unclean spirit which does not want that unsaved to become saved. However, there is no need for fear or hopelessness. Every believer has the power to bind the demons which are operating to block unsaved from surrendering to Jesus Christ.

You might be wondering what is meant by 'binding' demons. Before I explain that, let me deal with the 'sleeping demons' which attack you in an effort to hinder you from receiving the knowledge required to defeat all other unclean spirits. Take a minute; open your sanctified mouth and command the sleeping demon to get out of your body right now in Jesus name.

Change your position and repeat this command with authority: You sleeping demons, I command you to get out right now in the name of Jesus! You will not hinder me from reading this book! You will not hinder me from fulfilling my mandate to win souls for the kingdom of God. Out! Out! Out in Jesus' name! Now rest in the anointing which breaks yokes and sets captives free and let us continue our training as kingdom citizens.

Give God a praise for the victory! Glory! Hallelujah!

I trust you realize that this is real warfare. Yes, it is! This demon you just cast out is a very vicious one. However, his operations are very subtle. He is the same one who we encounter whenever we begin to pray. Have you ever felt the urge to pray and as soon as you begin, this demon rears its ugly head and sleep sets in from nowhere?

Can you recall having an experience with sleeping demons? You will realize that you do not really want to sleep because anything else with which you would have occupied yourself would not result in you being overcome by sleepiness. But the moment you take up your bible; the moment you begin to listen or watch some anointed preaching or teaching; the moment you begin to pray…Zzzzzzzzz! Sleep sets in. It is a sleeping demon! It has a close ally, the demon of drowsiness.

The Lord taught me an important lesson sometimes ago. He revealed to me that hell assigns two sets of demons to every pastor. One is a set of demons that blocks revelation and the other set includes the demon of drowsiness and sleepiness. These become very active as soon as the pastor begins to seek God for a word to bring to His people. Their responsibility is to hinder praying and studying the word of God. This is accomplished by employing distractions which hinders the pastor from being focused.

Warriors can you hear me? Are you hearing me warriors? This means that everyone involved in soul winning, must know how to bind these unclean spirits.

I will now continue with working at the altar. What do we mean to 'bind' a demon? The word 'bind' means 'to tie up'. It literally means 'to stop something or someone from functioning'. In other words, it means to block the unclean spirit from operating.

As outlined before, there are spirits which the devil has assigned to block the gospel. Paul said in 2 Corinthians 4:3-4

> *But if our gospel be hid, it is hid to them that are lost:*
> *In whom the god of this world hath blinded the minds of them which believe not, lest the light of the glorious gospel of Christ, who is the image of God, should shine unto them.*

There are unclean spirits which are called 'mind binding spirits' and 'will blocking spirits.' These spirits are released whenever someone wants to make a decision to serve God. They are manifesting whenever you hear persons make statements like these:

I want to serve God, but I don't know what is stopping me;

I know that I must serve the Lord, but I just cannot make up my mind to do it as yet;

I am not ready as yet.

All the above are as a result of the spirits in operation. Their aim is to block persons from making a decision to accept the gospel and serve God. This explains why a number of persons are still not saved. They remain bound by sin because whenever they visit a church or a ministry, the level of anointing present cannot bind those mind-binding and will-blocking demons. The persons therefore walk to the altar with a strong desire to be saved but cannot find the will-power to be saved.

This is an important area of spiritual warfare. As an altar worker, whenever you see someone approaching the altar, before you go to that person, bind the demon. You can do so by praying, "You demon in … (describe the person using clothing being worn or anything else significant, if you do not know the person's name) I bind you now! You will not function in the name of Jesus!"

This utterance immediately releases the power of God to incapacitate those unclean spirits. The angels which are released by your prayer, tie up those unclean spirits. Once they are bound, they are blocked from interfering with the person's will. The freedom is theirs at this point to accept the Lord as their personal Saviour.

While persons are at the altar and are being ministered to, there is another strategy that the unclean spirits use. This time their aim is to hinder the unbeliever from focusing on what is being said to them. This is done by throwing multiple thoughts at their minds, to lead them to a state of confusion. This will manifest in loss of focus, inability to pray and outright confusion. While he is throwing a barrage of thoughts at their minds, simultaneously, he is blocking their will.

When the minister of deliverance is operating in the Spirit realm, he cuts down all those activities as he stops the unclean spirits from functioning. Being now free from demonic influence, the unsaved persons now has the free will to choose whether to serve the Lord or to continue living in sin.

Altar workers do not need to be able to identify or call the demon in operation by name. Your responsibility is to ask the Lord to bind the unclean spirits operating as hindrances to the reconciliation of unsaved persons. That includes spirits working corporately or alone to block unbelievers from accepting Jesus as Lord and Saviour. Once you have prayed, the angels assigned to the altar knows them and will accomplish the task. Identifying demons by name is however, necessary while doing deliverance ministry.

Let me remind you of the importance of worship in both soul winning and deliverance ministries. In an atmosphere of intense worship, demons begin to manifest and sometimes subdued without much effort from a deliverance minister. Where the Shekinah Glory of God is being manifest in full force, deliverance is not being done in the laborious manner observed in some churches or ministries. True worship not only invokes the presence of God but paralyzes and renders demons powerless. At the command to leave, they have no option but to obey.

The reverse is true in atmospheres where the worship is not at a level where the presence and power of God is rich and potent. In such situations, sometimes hours are spent in prayer intended to cast out demons. This would not have been necessary where true worship has saturated the altar with God's presence. Remember that as the praises go up, the glory of God descends on His people. This make them potent. Nothing is impossible with God!

Binding the unclean spirits in preparation to ministering to someone at the altar is important. However, it is also very important for altar workers to know what to say as they approach an unbeliever at the altar.

The first thing to do is to greet the person warmly. 'Bless the Lord' is quite appropriate.

Secondly, you can enquire if the person is saved. If the answer is 'Yes' go on to ask if they were baptized in Jesus' name.

If the answer is 'No', you should then invite persons to give their life to the Lord. It is good to remind them of God's word which says that:

Now is the acceptable time, today if you hear My voice, harden not your heart.

As you continue to encourage persons to accept Jesus Christ as their personal Lord and Saviour, the conversation may include questions similar to these:

What do you think about giving your life to Jesus?

What do you think about being baptized today?

I think the Lord is ready for you; Are you ready for the Lord?

In the event that the unbeliever tells you that he/she is not ready as yet! In a calm, loving and caring manner, continue to entreat that soul by taking your questioning to the next level. An appropriate question at this point could be:

So, what are you waiting for?

Remind the person that the word of God says that 'Today is the day of salvation' then revert to the question:

So, why you do not want to accept the Lord?

If there is still a refusal to accept Jesus, as wisdom dictates, you could possibly ask if the person lives with an unmarried partner. Where appropriate, those questions become necessary because you would not want to take a woman who is living with her spouse and children, baptize her and send her back to live in the same condition.

There are certainly cases when the Spirit of the Lord moves in this manner! However, altar workers must be alert and know when to refer certain situations to higher authority. In most instances, this would be the Pastor, Elder or their designate. This is essential to ensure that Godly wisdom is being exercised in such cases. Be careful not to mislead persons into making inappropriate or foolish decisions! When in doubt, consult someone in authority! The leaders are expected to be equipped to interview these persons and advise them accordingly.

Warning! Altar workers please ensure that you do not threaten anyone because of your desire to get them baptized. Do not tell persons that if they do not get baptized, God is going to kill them! If God did not tell you that, you are lying! It is not about how many persons you lead to take water baptism. It is about how many persons truly surrender to the Lord and will eventually remain.

Jesus said that He expects our fruit to remain. Nothing is wrong if after you have led a person to Christ, you are told that he/she needs to go home and get things in order. There will definitely be instances when some important spiritual decisions must be made before baptism. In such cases, a contact number can be requested and used to communicate with the person as part of the following-up process. Continue to pray and fast for the individual, if you are so led. Once the person has resolved their issues, they will return and get into covenant with God through water baptism.

Pay keen attention altar workers! Be reminded that he that winneth souls is wise. You have to be knowledgeable and prepared to be effective in whichever area of ministry you labour. It is important to remain in the Spirit whenever you work at the altar.

Earlier, I told you that in witnessing, your gifts manifest. You will see the move of God in your life. You will begin to hear the voice of God. You will be led by the Spirit of God. You will find yourself knowing what to say; how to pray and when to pray. As the power of God uses you, the response from the person to whom you are witnessing will provide confirmation that God was using you.

There will be times when you are ministering to unbelievers and their responses are merely excuses. If you are in the Spirit, the Lord will reveal it and continue to give you guidance in continuing to minister until the person faces the truth and is persuaded to accept Jesus.

Tips for Altar Workers

Being an altar worker requires wisdom. When praying at the altar, be wise! Be careful not to push and shove persons at the altar. Do not harass persons by shaking them or rocking their heads to and fro. This is nothing but distraction to the unsaved. Whenever you are praying for an unsaved, there is no need for you to even put your hands on their heads. You should only do so by the leading of the Holy Spirit.

Female Altar Workers, I implore you to avoid placing your hands on a male's abdomen-belly, while praying with or for him. Bear in mind that the man you are praying for is a sinner. Had he been a Christian, it would be problematic. How much more that he is not? Touching an unsaved man in sensitive areas of his body is forbidden. You must be wise! Inappropriate physical contacts are distracting and amounts to nothing but sensual and sexual arousals.

Rubbing the male's chest, back or just about any part of his body as a female is improper. Some of these men will walk away from the altar with no godly encounter. The carnal mind then goes back to the streets and share stories belittling the ministry. It may vary from how they attended this or that church and a rather attractive sister from the church kissed their ear or how they were massaged. Women of God BE WISE!

Behold, I send you forth as sheep in the midst of wolves: be ye therefore wise as serpents, and harmless as doves. Matthew 10:16

In the absence of wisdom, those on the outside will view us as fanatics. Do not damage the reputation of the church by acting out of order. In like manner, brothers must avoid inappropriate physical contact with unsaved females, especially while praying with and for them. They should even exercise more caution, since some of these women are either married or in intimate relationships. Brothers could be accused of not only offending the females, but also their partners. Be warned! Limit body contact and wherever possible, make none at all.

Whenever you are praying, you must also exercise wisdom. Do not tightly close your eyes and pray without remaining alert. Be watchful and prayerful at the same time. Remain in the Spirit of the Lord with a consciousness that witnessing is warfare. While praying for someone, demons within them could instruct them to physically hurt you. Being alert would give you an advantage over impending dangers.

I recall incidents in which unclean spirits instruct persons to hurt altar workers. Once, a fourteen year old girl, smote an evangelist in the face and lifted a pastor causing him to free-fall to the ground. This she did with only one hand; she then looked at them and laughed. I have witnessed unsaved viciously remove the hands of altar workers from off them during prayer. In each situation, after being delivered, the persons stated that they were not conscious of those actions. I said it before, the altar is a dreadful place! It is a war zone!

I have heard christians cry out 'wooh!' right at the altar. This resulted from pain inflicted when unclean spirits instructed an unsaved to grab the hair of the altar worker. She obeyed and pull the altar worker's hair with such great intensity that excruciating pain was experienced. The altar is a dangerous place!

There is no place to fight fleshy wars at the altar. Demons will humiliate altar workers. I still remember the impression on the evangelist face today. She wanted so badly to retaliate. However, she exercised restraint knowing that it was not the child's natural behaviour but the work of the enemy.

Why am I saying all of this?
Be ready for war when you come to the altar!
Be alert!
Be led by the Spirit of God!
Be prayerful!
Be watchful!
That which will be done at the altar is:

Not by might, nor by power, but by My Spirit, saith the Lord of Hosts. Zechariah 4:6

Chapter 9

BYWAYS AND HEDGES

The Lord teaches soul winners. If we continue to be led, eventually we will be empowered to do the very things that the Lord uses other anointed leaders to do. Adherence to the Spirit of God, including what He has led me to share in this handbook, assist us in becoming all that God ordained us to be in His kingdom.

The manifested power of God is not displayed in a believer's life overnight. Rather it grows from level to level as we endeavor to fulfil our purpose within the body of Christ. Entering the byways and hedges to witness is perfect opportunity for the gifts of the Spirit to manifest.

Let me hasten to inform you that the altar is quite different from the byways and hedges. In distinguishing one from the other, I would liken the byways and hedges to the enemy's territory-the battlefield, while inside the church is like the army base.

Although war goes on in both zones, they are of varying magnitude and nature. There is also a greater advantage in fighting within the army base. It is usually a much safer zone, where the battle is already won and with fewer causalities. This is generally true with the exception of isolated cases where the enemy hits the army base unexpectedly.

At the point which an unsaved comes to church, some demons have already been defeated. However, when you go out to witness, you have gone to interfere with the set of demons who hinders them from coming to the house of God also. That is reason for you not to worry as they approach the altar. The devil has already been defeated to an extent!

On the contrary, witnessing in the byways and hedges, lands you right in the heart of the territories where demons are in total control. Your presence is direct interference with the kingdom of darkness. You are right in the enemy's camp!

But guess what?
THERE IS NO NEED TO FEAR!

There is no reason to be afraid at all! At all! At all! The word of God gives us confidence in 1John 4:4

> *Ye are of God, little children, and have overcome them: because greater is He that is in you, than he that is in the world.*

VERY IMPORTANT NOTICE FOR SOUL WINNERS:

Your primary purpose is to lead unbelievers into personal relationships with Jesus Christ.

DO NOT force persons to take water baptism.

Through prayer, bind the unclean spirits hindering unbelievers from accepting Jesus freely.

Being free, unbelievers will make a decision, free from demonic interference.

Whenever you go out to the byways and hedges, observe the principles outlined for altar workers, while not ignoring the ones written more specifically for that environment. This is a more intense war zone! This is the real battlefield!

Be ready for war!

Be informed!

Be prepared!

Study your Bible and this handbook!

Fast and pray!

Go in the Spirit and power of Almighty God!

There is no need for fear with Jesus as our Commander in Chief! Listen to Him and obey whatever He tells you to do! Follow His instructions carefully and allow Him to teach you warfare. Remember that you are not able to run back and forth to the army base for advice and your Pastor, Elder, Youth leader, Men's or Women's president might not be in close proximity. Most importantly, God is with you! Let the Omnipotent, Omnipresent and Omniscient One direct you.

Before you engage in any form of soul-winning exercise, it is important to pray for God's leading and direction. Witnessing and altar working are for all believers. Together we complete the mission, not compete on the mission. There will be embarrassing encounters, even with other believers who want to show their greatness and your smallness.

My word to you is simply this:

LET NO ONE BREAK YOUR SPIRIT!

Whenever you are humiliated by believers while on the mission field, be comforted in the fact that it is not right; neither does the church condone it. However, **do not resort to self-defense** and **do not get discouraged**. Complete the mission! Never run from battle!

On returning safely to the army base, fast, pray and continue to avail yourself to God to be used in soul winning. If the situation necessitates, report it to the leader or his designate for intervention. Our reaction in these and all other trying circumstances, is indicative of our level of christian maturity.

It is godly to relax instead of retaliate! On the other hand, as you remain calm, the character of the offender is being exposed. Warriors, being led by the Spirit of God, will not intentionally wound his fellow soldier.

However, if there is retaliation, the enemy has overcome both the offender and the offended.

When we are being led by the same Spirit, things will be done decently, in order and in proper timing. Where there is chaos, anarchy and hostility towards each other, the flesh is usually at work. Remember to stay in the Spirit!

There are instances when persons act out of zeal to see others saved and some persons would have been offended by their actions. Remember that we should cover each other's actions with love. Our love and desire to win souls for the kingdom, does not make us flawless in character. As we work together, let humility, love, honour and respect for our fellow soldier guide our actions. It would not be wise for us to win souls on the battlefield and destroy our brothers and sisters in the process. This would mean replacing citizens in the kingdom instead of allowing the kingdom to grow numerically.

As I pointed out in Chapter Five of my second book, 'The Leader Who Covers', war sometimes occur in strange places, the church being no exemption. The greatest victory that the enemy gets is when he sets believers at war among themselves. The devil's kingdom is not divided so it advances forcefully. Likewise, if the kingdom of God is to overthrow the kingdom of darkness, it has to observe and employ the strategy the enemy is using against believers. We must be wise as a serpent but harmless as a dove. **Do not divide! Unite!**

The Elder of our church pointed out during a teaching session that there have been times when parents are reported to have uttered unpleasant things to their children; not realizing that the children would have naturally found the utterances hurtful. He further pointed out that, at times, these hurt continue years after the incidents.

This is just as true with parents in the Lord as with biological parents. Nonetheless, children of God should strive to be at a certain dimension in God, that even when they are hurt, they are open to receive healing. This is a prerequisite for spiritual growth and development.

Who is the healer?
Jesus is the Healer!

Fortunately, we do not need to spend our limited financial resources to secure the professional services of psychologists and psychiatrists. Hurting saints serve a God who Paul describes this way in Hebrews 4:15

> *For we have not an high priest which cannot be touched with the feeling of our infirmities; but was in all points tempted like as we are, yet without sin.*

Clearly, being hurt is inevitable but we need to go to Jesus and place the situation in His capable hands. It is quite in order to pour out everything to Him. Let Him know exactly what was done to you and how it made you feel. In the process, release the source of hurt through forgiveness and ask the Lord to heal you. You will be amazed at the power of forgiveness and how quickly God restores you, in order for you to finish the mission.

The enemy will do anything to hinder us from winning souls. We must be knowledgeable of how to quickly resolve issues among ourselves and continue to work. Regardless of the origin of the attack we face as believer, the promise of God remains the same in Isaiah 54:17:

> *No weapon that is formed against thee shall prosper, and every tongue that shall rise against thee in judgment thou shalt condemn. This is the heritage of the servants of the Lord, and their righteousness is of me, saith the Lord.*

This is true whether the weapon is formed without or within. Note that the word of God declares that EVERY TONGUE that rise against thee in judgment, thou shalt condemn.

Did you hear that?
EVERY TONGUE!
EVERY TONGUE!
EVERY TONGUE!

You must realize that whatever the tongue says against you, God has given you the right to speak over it. God is not the One who will condemn the tongue which speaks judgmental words to destroy you. You are the one who must condemn them. Neither is it the tongues that rise against you, it is every one of them! Therefore, do not be discouraged or distracted by unpleasant circumstances.

There might just be an embarrassing moment when in witnessing to someone, you told them something, believing that you heard from the Lord. Afterward, according to the person's response, you discovered that you were so wrong. Do not let that hinder you from continuing to be a witness. Whether it was a simple statement or something as serious as, "God says you were diagnosed with cancer," and the person denies it and declares publicly, "I have no idea what you are talking about. Stop telling lies on God!" Do not allow even such humiliation to stop you from getting back to the altar and praying for others.

Have you observed that at times those who are seemingly powerful in the church, retreats whenever the church steps out of its comfort zone and enters the streets? Clearly some warriors become afraid once they get into the byways and hedges. They are overcome by timidity; being intimidated by the unclean spirits of these territories. To these warriors, God's word says,

"For God hath not given us the spirit of fear; but of power, and of love, and of a sound mind." 2 Timothy 1:7

I realize though that God has kept His word to me and is recruiting an army of brave soldiers for these end times. Whenever they go into the streets, being in right standing with God, they will take over the enemy's territory and deliver those who are bound in Jesus' name.

Warriors, where are you?

Do not retreat on the battlefield. Stand flatfooted and face the enemy in the power and Spirit of God. Whenever the church takes to the streets, step out boldly, lay hands on the unbelievers and pray for them. You are not alone! Other warriors are with you. So too are your spiritual leaders who can provide additional support for you as you engage in a new dimension of warfare. Do not copy the behaviour of those warriors who will only take on the demons that are already bound in the confines of the church walls. Real warriors are not afraid of the demons in the streets!

Chapter 10

CONDUCT OF CHRIST'S AMBASSADORS

When Jesus sent His disciples on the street, note that He said,

> *"Behold, I send you forth as sheep in the midst of wolves: be ye therefore wise as serpents, and harmless as doves."*

Your approach to witnessing in the streets cannot be as though you are lions. Your approach should rather be sheep-like; humble.

This is still no reason to be fearful. Do not worry that you are behaving as sheep among wolves because the lion is still there inside each warrior. Be calm! Be wise! You should not approach unbelievers with a boisterous, condemnatory spirit. Instead, approach them with a spirit of meekness, humility, love and compassion for the lost. Those are character traits of a sheep and a dove.

Never forget this! As you go, go with the wisdom of God. Whenever you approach unbelievers in this manner, you will experience a spirit of acceptance. The people of this world are in search of peace and will therefore readily open their spirit to the gospel which you desire to present. The spirit of humility that you display will also be something that they admire and crave after. The world is looking for peace, joy, love and hope. Persons who are peaceful also carry joy, so they will find you attractive and your message appealing.

Members, as well as church leaders, carry different levels of anointing. Believers are also anointed for different areas of ministry. Do not compare yourselves with each other. Do not compete with each other. Unite and complete the work of the kingdom. Let us reach the lost at any cost. Never lose sight of the ultimate goal which is to colonize the world that Christ becomes all in all.

The Apostle Mark was anointed to pastor the church, while Apostle Peter was anointed to open doors. He was the key-man. The Apostle John the beloved carried the anointing to write the book of Revelation. Yet, John the Baptist carried the anointing to be at the river, baptizing as he prepared the way for Jesus. Enough said to substantiate the statement that we are all uniquely anointed. In the same manner that each person has a unique fingerprint, whenever the anointing sits on each believer, there is a specific job within the kingdom of God that the person is anointed to accomplish.

Wisdom is the principal thing! Regardless of how anointed you are, whenever you go into the streets to minister -individually or as a group- you will not be able to win souls by speaking in tongues. Whenever I am anointed to preach, the Spirit of the Lord resting on me, gives me wisdom to deliver the word suitable for the territory in which I am placed.

This is one of the reasons why I continue to reiterate that we must remain and operate under the leading of the Spirit of God. We cannot ignore this instruction and be effective in advancing the kingdom of God. If you operate foolishly, you are not ministering, you are performing. Eventually, those who you want to win will end up making mockery of your performance. Allowing the Spirit of God to lead, will result in you being able to deliver the word in a timely and convincing manner, leading to repentance.

Let me hasten to say that during witnessing, believers reveal the quality of substance within them. Some people are always speaking in tongues, but they do not know the word of God. During witnessing, they will be ashamed; not being able to rightly divide the word of truth. Therefore, Apostle Paul admonished Timothy, his son in the faith:

> *Study to shew thyself approved unto God, a workman that needeth not to be*

ashamed, rightly dividing the word of truth 2 Timothy 2:15.

A scenario is painted in the Church of Corinth which Apostle Paul had to address in 1Corinthians 14. This is the church cited as the most gifted in Church history yet Paul had to admonish them at length on how to operate in speaking in unknown tongues in the church. How much more important it is to pay attention to his advice in the streets, where all the people around are unbelievers. Believers who consider themselves too anointed to sit and learn these things, are the main ones whose behaviour in the streets bring the church into disrepute. Their ignorant actions allow unbelievers to make a mockery of the ministry to which they are attached.

Wise believers not only win souls. These believers also study to be able to present the gospel in a manner which brings God glory and advances His kingdom. With such individuals God is well pleased.

The bible teaches that the spirit of the prophet is subject to the prophet. This means that the gift that God has placed within us, is not uncontrollable. Therefore, during the manifestation of the gift, nothing foolish ought to be forthcoming.

Do not mistake what I am addressing, with the ignorance of unbelievers to the things of God. This does not refer to the confusion experienced by the unsaved whenever God uses the foolish things of this world to confound the wise.

The gifts which God gives to believers are manifested through the Spirit of God. It follows therefore, that a gifted believer- being led by the Spirit of God- ought to know how to operate in different settings. Christ Ambassadors should be wise enough to know when to do what. Paul said it like this:

> *"For though I be free from all men, yet have I made myself servant unto all, that I might gain more.*
>
> *And unto the Jews I became as a Jew, that I might gain the Jews, to them that are under the law, as under the law, that I might gain them that are under the law;*
>
> *To them that are without law, as without law, (being not without law to God, but under the law to Christ), that I might gain them that are without law.*
>
> *To the weak became I as weak, that I might gain the weak: I am made all things to all men, that I might by all means save some."* 1 Corinthians 9:19-22

Notice how flexible Paul was in his ministry, yet without compromising the gospel or quenching the Spirit of God. To the Romans, he operated like a Roman. To the Jews, he behaved like a Jew; at one point shaving his head and keeping the feast of the Passover. All this was done with one aim, to win souls for the kingdom of God. That's wisdom!

The spirit that God gives to believers is a spirit of wisdom. In this spirit resides the power to transform, not just to win people to Christ. Any witnessing team that is going to present Christ to the world, must be led by persons who are wise. These leaders must be so wise that they know who to call on to pray in which environment.

Paul pointed out that unless this Godly wisdom is exercised, our ministry will be ineffective. In addressing the matter of speaking in tongues, he admonished believers that even though we speak in much tongues and it reaches to heaven, the people around us will not have been ministered to. Instead of being edified, they would have become confused.

I trust that every Spirit filled believer who desires to be fruitful, invests some quality time in studying and observing to do the things God has led me to highlight here. Sadly, many believers who speak in tongues do not know how to operate outside of that experience. I will repeat for emphasis. Many believers who speak in tongues do not know how to operate in any other setting other than when they are speaking in tongues.

If you think that I am lying, observe these persons when someone is reading the bible in a service. Shortly after someone begins to read the text, these persons begin to speak in tongues so loudly that it prevents congregants from hearing the word being read. Now, the Spirit of God does not operate in such a manner. The Spirit of God is not the author of confusion.

At the time allotted for Praise and Worship, everyone is free to worship and pray aloud in tongues. However, whenever the Bible is being read, someone is testifying, praying or preaching, it is important that order and decency be displayed so that those who are not of the faith can hear and be edified. Not just those which are without, believers also need to hear for edification of their souls too.

Believers, do not erupt in speaking in tongues, disrupting the service and then say that you were operating under the influence of the Holy Ghost. Do not bring the ministry into disrepute by your ignorance and then claim you were under the anointing or that the Holy Ghost had taken you over. This ought not to be! There is a proper time for everything in the church and everything must be done decently and in order. The same is true when you go into the streets or other places of worship. Know your environment and be wise in your operations. You are God's representatives! Represent well!

Should you, in the process of outdoor witnessing enter the home of someone who believes in tongues, as you pray and worship with that individual, tongues are quite in order. It is something that will edify this individual. By all means, go ahead and pray in tongues. That's wisdom too!

In a home where the people do not believe in tongues or understand tongues, endeavor not to get off into speaking too much tongues. Do not get me wrong! There will be times when the power of the Holy Ghost sits upon a believer and there is nothing that should be done to hinder the Spirit of God from operating in whatever way He chooses.

In that case, obedience to the Spirit of God is wisdom in full operation. Let God have His way! Tongues and all! In this atmosphere, under the unction of the Holy Ghost, you might even find yourself moving around the environment. My God! Every demon has to back up, retreat and surrender! Hallelujah!

Consequently, the power of God on full display, will lead unbelievers to request baptism in Jesus name. Recently, I was preaching at a church on invitation, when I delivered the word the believers praised God. However, as the Spirit of the Lord shifted me into the prophetic realm, I called out a few persons from the congregation and told them what God had shown me. Afterwards I said, "There is a young man on the outside who needs to come for prayer. Come now!"

Immediately several young men began walking into the church in single file. At the end of the service, thirteen persons walked straight to the pool and were baptized in Jesus' name. Most of them were the young men who came for prayer. What do you think happened? Nothing but the power of the Holy Ghost in operation wrought conviction in them. All I am saying is that we must be led by the Spirit of God and be wise.

Whenever you are praying as a group for an unsaved, someone leads in prayer, while the others come in agreement with the person praying. Allow the Spirit of God to have His way. I cannot overemphasize that point. We are labourers with Christ and He is our Commander in Chief. Follow His directives and victory is guaranteed!

While you are praying as a group, something could be revealed through the Spirit to another person in the group. Remember that the spirit of the prophet is subject to the prophet. Wait until the person is through praying and then you proceed with sharing as the Spirit of God leads. This will avoid any confusion.

Remember to be obedient to the one who God places over you. We trust God and pray for leaders who are wise and are led by God. Whenever they give instructions to mission teams, make sure you obey. Whenever the person directs the group to stop, everyone should stop and whenever the group is directed to go, everyone should go. Move with the flow and follow the group leader's instructions. Anyone who disobeys, sins. This kind of rebellion against spiritual authority, opens doors for attacks from the devil. The battlefield is not a place for power struggle! United we stand; divided we fall.

Be careful to stay together on the battlefield. Do not lag to take on any task while the group has moved on. The bible says:

> *Be sober, be vigilant, because your adversary the devil, as a roaring lion,*

walketh about, seeking whom he may devour 1 Peter 5:8.

Have you ever observed the operations of lions? If they come upon a herd of buffalos, they roar ferociously, driving fear into the animals and send them running. If the buffalos remain together, the lions cannot defeat them. However, if in the process of running, any buffalo strays or gets left behind; it becomes an easy target for the enemy to defeat.

The same is true as Christian warriors. We must stick together in obedience, not only for our witnessing to be effective but also for our safety. If the lions attempted to attack the herd, without a doubt, they would be struck through with their horns and trampled upon. There is no way for the lions to defeat a herd of buffalos.

This is what the enemy wants to accomplish whenever we enter the mission field as a group. He wants to divide the group. He wants to separate us to weaken our power against him. When any of the believers stray or lag in disobedience, giving in to distractions or by discouragement; the enemy swoops in to make a kill. Be careful! Follow the leader and be in obedience; Go with the flow! Move with the army!

Remember that you do not go out on the byways and hedges to live. We are out there to plant a seed. Plant the seed and keep moving. At the end of planting, head home to be refreshed and replenished.

Some persons have been taught that you must be on fasting while you are ministering outside of the church. This includes witnessing in streets, visits to hospitals, infirmaries, prison ministry and so on. Personally, I have been taught by the Lord that the enemy from time to time, releases teachings to instill fear of demons in the hearts of believers. I believe this is one such teaching.

Let me quickly clarify my point. Nothing is wrong with fasting and witnessing, if you are so led. However, contrary to what the enemy would want us to believe and be fearful, is the declaration of God's word:

> *Ye are of God, little children and have overcome them: because greater is He that is in you, than he that is in the world*
> 1John 4:4.

Most importantly, the mission is what God has chosen us for. This is the purpose for which we were brought into the kingdom.

The enemy would want to intimidate believers to hinder them from doing the work of the Lord. Because they are being taught to anticipate the backlash of demons, they will be hesitant to engage in altar work or going out on the battlefield.

It is good to fast! Personally, I do not fast when I am going on the battlefield to preach the word. There are exceptions, such as, whenever I am on fasting and the Lord instructs me to go. I do not fast to go out for more than one reason.

Firstly, I am a soldier and I am already prepared for war. Listen carefully, I am not saying that you cannot go on fasting whenever you are going out. However, I would not teach it as a doctrine that you must be on fasting to go out and minister.

Secondly, there are missions on which I go that I am unable to fast. Wisdom dictates that fasting would be inappropriate due to the nature of the warfare in which I would be engaged and the type of people with whom I would be socializing.

There are also situations where refusing what is being offered to eat and drink is considered insulting. Wisdom must be exercised in each situation. I reiterate, as I have echoed numerous times before in this handbook, 'Be led by the Spirit of God' This is key!

Whenever I am called to minister, it is sometimes a blessing to the persons who cater to my needs. They are fulfilled by the fact that they were able to feed God's servant. There are some places you will go to minister and the Lord may want you to have a drink of water there. Other places the Lord might want you to have even a soda or something to eat. So only if you are led, you must fast, while on outdoor ministry.

You could also fast ahead of the time scheduled for outdoor ministry. In this case, you could refresh yourselves just before going out to minister. Remember too, that you need energy, depending on the type of ministry in which you are about to engage. Usually, a high level of physical energy is exerted in preaching and deliverance ministries. Again, I say, unless I am led by the Spirit of God -who is able to sustain me- it would be foolish to go on fasting while I am engaging in these battles.

Another important thing is that as you minister, keep covering yourself under the blood of Jesus. If you have bad dreams or experiences of attacks in the spiritual realm, destroy it in the name of Jesus. Constantly pray for blood coverage in the name of Jesus.

As a warrior, use all your tools both in preparation for warfare, and while you are in the heat of battle. Be patient, compassionate, loving and kind. Do not get anxious! The saving of the soul is ultimately in God's hand. Do your part and leave the rest to Him.

At this point, if you have not yet read my first book, WARRING UNCLEAN SPIRITS, I implore you to do so. If it has been a while since you read it, now might be a great time to reread it in preparation to fulfill your kingdom mandate.

This is a new dimension warriors! Having been reconciled to God, it is your turn to engage in the ministry of reconciliation.

This handbook is a tool to help in preparing you to be wise and effective soul winners. As you increase in knowledge and understanding by its reading, be sure to increase your impact on the kingdom of darkness by wisely applying its principles and guidelines.

Apostle Winston G. Baker

LET US GO AND COLONIZE OUR WORLD IN THE NAME OF JESUS!

WELCOME TO THE NEXT LEVEL CHRIST'S AMBASSADORS!

www.ingramcontent.com/pod-product-compliance
Lightning Source LLC
Chambersburg PA
CBHW061450040426
42450CB00007B/1299